MAYRA−ALEJANDRA ALVARADO

Sharod−Azarian
and His Hamster Named
Mouse!

AuthorHouse™
1663 Liberty Drive
Bloomington, IN 47403
www.authorhouse.com
Phone: 833-262-8899

This book is printed on acid-free paper.

ISBN: 978-1-6655-3531-1 (sc)
ISBN: 978-1-6655-3532-8 (e)

Print information available on the last page.

Published by AuthorHouse 08/17/2021

authorHOUSE

Sharod-Azarian and his Hamster Named Mouse!

As the Hamster arrived at its new home.

There in the home lives this little boy named Sharod—Azarian, who is so happy and excited, for his new pet.

That as soon as the hamster arrived—he named him Mouse.

Sharod—Azarian began petting and playing with Mouse.

This little boy took Mouse on an airplane ride.

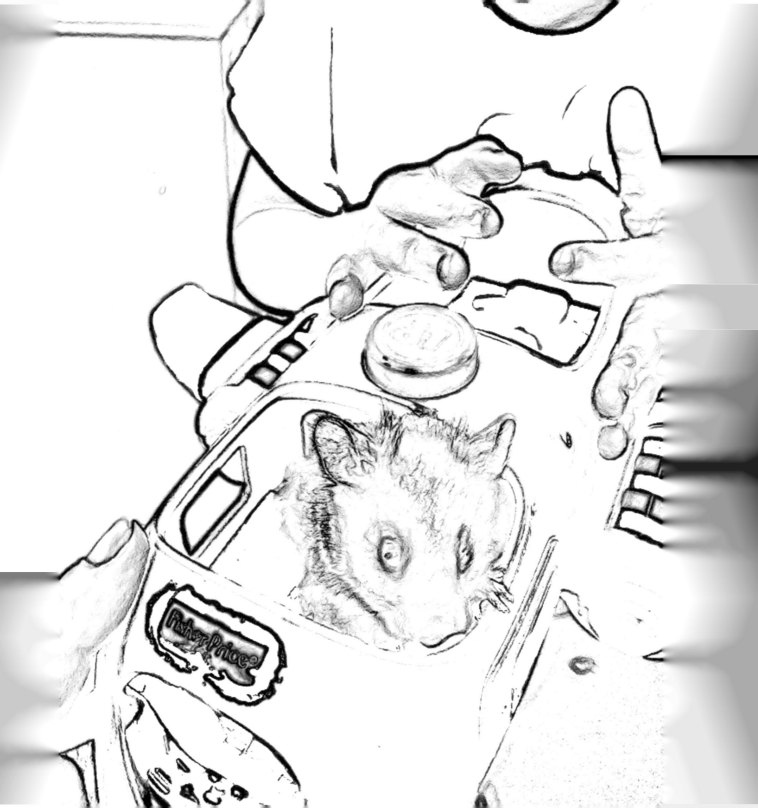

He gave mouse a clear upscale view of his entire home.

Then Sharod—Azarian took Mouse
in a bus ride, front row seat.

He began pushing Mouse
all through the home.

Mouse got a first-class yellow bus ride.

Sharod-Azarian is having so much fun with Mouse.

momma began saying to him, "let us put Mouse in his cage."

Sharod-Azarian said, "No! this my mouse. I want to play."

"Mouse is sleepy." Momma said.

"Mouse do not want to play anymore." He put the hamster down on the carpet.

Mouse ran into the kitchen and underneath the refrigerator.

Sharod—Azarian feels sad now and says

"You don't want to play with me?"
While he searches for Mouse.

Sharod—Azarian said, "Momma,
please find Mouse."

The he said, "Please please
please find my mouse."

As he walks away, he called,

"Mouse! Mouse! Mouse!" But he could not find him. "Momma momma help me." "Ok. I will look and listen."

He grabs a pillow, to sit down on and crossed his legs, closed his eyes.

Creating full silence,

hoping that Mouse will come out and play.

Now momma could not find Mouse neither.

Later, in the night Mouse
came out from hiding.

Momma pick Mouse up, and she place the hamster in Sharod—Azarian hands. He is feeling so happy again. He then decided to read Mouse a story about hamsters.

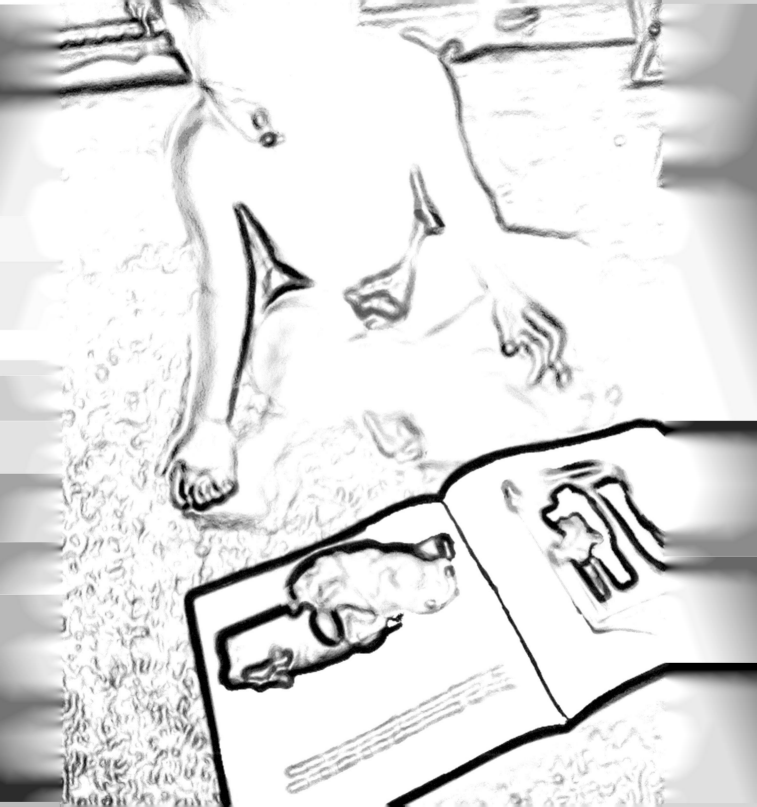

After the story he took Mouse on one more ride around on top of his head.

before putting him back in his cage. I love you Mouse. Goodnight Mouse.

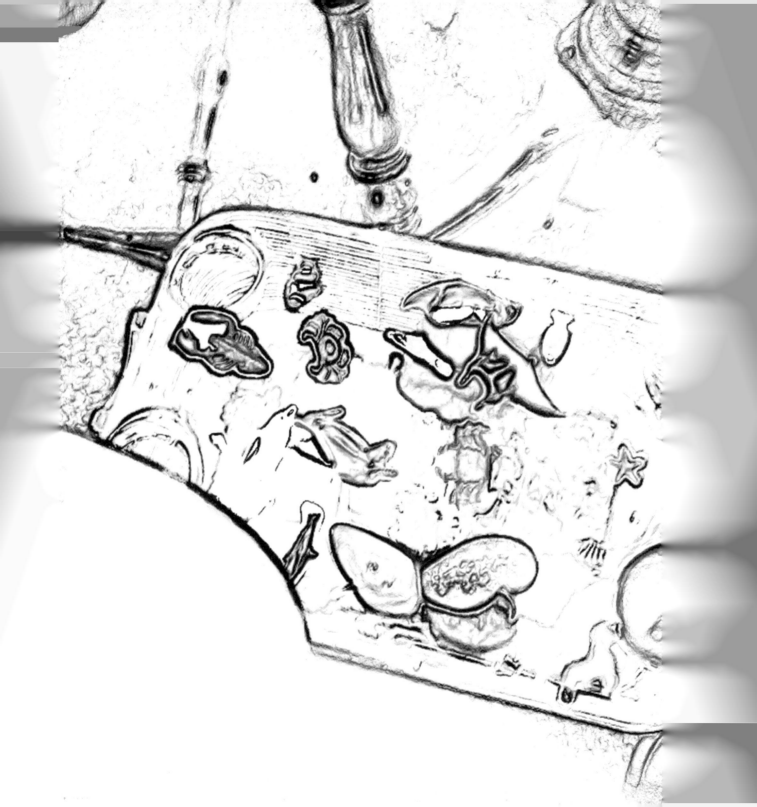

Printed in the United States
by Baker & Taylor Publisher Services